Simple Academic Overviews:
Vol. 1, 2 & 3

Dr. Jenice Armstead

Simple Academic Overviews

Vol. 1, 2 & 3

6" x 9" (15.24 x 22.86 cm)
Black & White on Cream paper
58 pages
ISBN-13: 978-1522880172 (CreateSpace-Assigned)
ISBN-10: 1522880178
BISAC: Business & Economics / General

Disclaimer

The reader should use their own judgment in utilizing the information in this book. The reader should seek advice from professionals as needed. The author's advice and information are based on professional experiences The author/publisher shall have neither responsibility nor liability to any person or entity with respect to any damages directly or indirectly as an aspect by any advice or information contained herein.

Dedication

This book series is dedicated to knowledge hungry students, academic knowledge workers, educators and motivators of the business and business related fields.

Continue to Empower Others,
Dr. Jenice Armstead

Photo Credit: Davina McGinnis

TABLE OF CONTENTS

Biography

Dr. Jenice Armstead is a military veteran, author, motivational speaker, Professor and Academic Business Department Chair with over 17 years professional experience in the public and private sector. Jenice's expertise covers human resources, business management, the federal hiring process and government hiring policy. She understands the significance of human capital value for organizational development. She has an exceptional aptitude for teaching difficult topics with practical approaches. Jenice has a MBA with a Concentration in Human Resources from Saint Leo University and a Doctorate of Business Administration from Jones International University.

Introduction

This section provides an historical overview of the development of management principles during the Scientific Management Era. Including key scholars, principles, and insights, as well as notable critiques of scientific management. Human resources managers today, explain principles of scientific management as the topics are related to organizational policy, organizational development and also promote organizational growth.

The scientific management era began during World War II, in the United States and spread abroad which allowed organizations to implement necessary changes to businesses practices along with developing usable management practices for organizations. The United States Government set laws and policies in place, and proclaimed scientific management principles into the industrial workforce. With the economy at an all time down fall, scientific management examined business progression and focused on evolution of policy development with an emphasis on workforce improvement and performance management productivity. Industrial and labor relations took the lead in keeping in greater profession where management often was represented. The scientific management era outlined the need for developing operational policies, determining business objectives and goals for creating a stronger workforce.

Scientific Management Era

Scientific management historically gives relevance to the industrial era by precisely outlining ambivalence to the jurisdiction of shifting management thoughts to new ways of analyzing business practices. The scientific management era of thought is more than implementing policies and regulations; it gives understanding of the importance of human capital as a key business relation. There was a need to strive for the highest degree of productivity for not only the employee, but for the organization as a whole. In order for organizations to be productive, scientific management era developed organizational policy and structures to assist with organizational development by improving the competitive edge of a business. The principles of the scientific management era ascertained environmental uncertainty for businesses. The newly developed principles allowed for organizations to influence positive changes for organizational structure.

Scientific Management Era: Key Scholars, Principles, and Insights

The Father of Scientific Management, Fredrick W. Taylor, revolutionized the workforce by greatly influencing the scientific management era and changing business management thought of the workplace. Taylor's achievements in scientific management effectively educated business owners by revealing the "business influence" based on principles from "The Course of American Democratic Thought." Taylor discusses scientific management and business development for organizational profitability (Rowlinson, 1988).

The thought behind the scientific management era was to turn out a higher quality of work, but the catch was businesses had to pay employees more. The principles increase competitiveness, and allows for organizations to stay current in an ever-changing business market (Freedman, 1950).

Organizational structure is everything. Take for example fast food chains; they work much like the scientific management era functioned. Each fast food chain has an exact business structure for how food is prepared, how long it should take for the customer to receive their food and the quality of their food being served to customers. The fast food industry competition is stiff, and a "meal deals" are a dime a dozen, the key is to ensure the prices are low enough to still be competitive to keep the customer coming back. This is where scientific management comes in the picture. Scientific management is objective, it allows for numerous business methods to be analyzed and evaluated based on the benefits as they relate to what "works" and what "doesn't work" for the organization. This is the reason why some fast food companies have survived, and competitors have conquered others.

Organizational Policy

As a human resource professional, implementing an organizational policy of "science of work" is one of the scientific management approaches that give a fresh management thought to "old ways" of doing things. When an employee is motivated to work using a positive method verses a negative method, the employee results will be different. Using the "science of work" takes the management compensation principle, and changes the focus to the employee. For example, organizational structures, which base compensation on, hours worked are a standardized way for employees to understand how their wages are earned. But, if an employee has options for compensation other than working a set amount of hours, the results are more favorable. "Teleworking" is an excellent way to motivate employees to work; while working from home is not an option for all organizations it is an employee benefit when implementing "science of work" into organizational policy. If an organization implemented an organizational policy of "Teleworking" for employees to work, the amount of hours worked would not seem as stressful for the employee. By supplying employee's options to take care of personal items while using a "Teleworking" schedule as an alternative to coming into work everyday, this works as a motivational tool. Implementing new organizational policy is a win-win for the entire organization, along with keeping moral high. Scientific management evolves a vast array of aspects such as using "Teleworking" schedules to focus on organizational development.

Training and development is another benefit to the organizational policy implementation. Training and development of employees gives employees a sense of belonging. When employees feel they are apart of an organization, their work performance will increase. Training and development empowers employees to grow professionally, and strengthens the employee/management relationship by showing the employee their value in the organization. Training and development ensures all efforts from the organization are directed toward a common goal of promoting excellence for the employee. In order for an organization to acquire a healthy structured foundation, employee value needs to be substantiated. Businesses have the ability to grow and gradually develop training programs with using techniques such as computer-based training. The key concept in implementation of any training and development program involves communication with employees. With the policy development focused on employee value, organizations secure their longevity among their competitors.

Conclusion

Understanding the importance of implementing scientific management principles pertains to organizational policy development, implementation and step-by-step follow through. There are many ways to implement changes that consist of low difficulty levels for employees to adjust quickly to the changes. In all fairness, scientific management is highly objective, organizational policy starts with businesses laying the foundation for how employees will be expected to preform.

Truth be told, the "scientific management" approach is a natural part of management, which can be oversimplified if not developed and implemented correctly (Freedman, 1950). The implemented methods give indicating factors of problems, along with grounding ways to solve those problems. Management's understanding of problems within the business gives the business an

immediate competitive edge over peer businesses.

Introduction

This section provides the understanding of the concepts of performance management is related to organizational development theory. Includes a description and critique of at least four key strategies of performance management. Human resource professionals are the point of contacts for explaining how to support organizational development through application of performance management strategies.

Performance management is critical to all organization and employee success. Organizational development theory measures the criteria for the development of organizations. Both performance management and organizational development theory encompass product quality, time management and strategic focus. The close link between performance management and organizational development theory evolves analyzing the pressures of global business factors to include social, legal and technological business aspects. The concepts of performance management and organizational development theory work systematically together.

Preformance Management Related to Organizational Development Theory

Performance management and organizational development theory are directly related to workforce composition and the business contributions of diverse workers. Using the framework of performance management, organizational development theory engages the organization by enhancing the performance factors of individuals. For example, performance management of employees breaks down the knowledge required of the employee or the position, guidelines for conducting the job, the scope and effect of the job, and the physical/mental/ ability of the employee to work in the job. Organizational development theory takes the breakdown, and applies managerial aspects to the business concept for carrying out the responsibilities for the job to be preformed (Wheeler, 2000). A goal of performance management is to achieve the necessary results for the organization to develop future profits. Performance management and organizational development theory both have roles within an organizational foundation, directly related to the needs and conduct of business practices. The concept of performance management and organizational development theory can undergo levels of change within an organization. Performance management aimlessly ensures the organization is working together for the optimum results of achieving profits, as organizational development uses the results of performance management for organizational develop (Wheeler, 2000).

Organizational Change Strategy

Organizational change strategy is needed in order to implement performance metrics of an organization. What has the organization been doing? What has worked for the organization? What hasn't worked for the organization? Are employees satisfied with their work-life? How are promotions decided for employees? Are the job descriptions correct? These are all questions to be asked when implementing organizational change strategies based on performance management. For example, organizational change strategies in popular retail stores evolved taking a hard look at their competitors. Retail stores thrive off of performance management changes such as how products were displayed for customers, customer service improvements and great prices for customers. Change is everything; change is what organizations need to grow and develop. Organizations are finding change ensures longevity in the global market.

Performance Management System Strategy

The performance management system strategy takes into account how performance management is evaluated for the organization. The performance management system strategy consists of analyzing shareholder value and identifying issues within the organization. This involves senior managers developing new practices, communicating performance expectations for employees, and defining different activities to enhance the organizational development processes.

Performance management system strategy provides feedback, which is used as a comprehensive approach to measuring the success of implemented business tactics (Witt, 2000). For example, performance management system strategy of evaluation of employees must show employee development or improvement. Without the ability to measure employee performance, an organization has no idea if the employee is profitable or not for the organization.

Implementation Strategy

Implementation strategy of performance management evolves senior management to contribute to the success of the performance management system strategy. Implementation strategy is used as a tool for organizational development after performance management system strategy is analyzed by the organization (Witt, 2000). Implementation strategy aligns with the change and performance management systems strategies, giving human resources useful practices to improve organizational structure. During the implementation strategy, employees have a tendency to show resistance. Making sure there are step-by-step instructions for how implementation will be conducted for the organization will ease any employee resistance that may occur. The key to the implementation strategy is to gradually conduct the implementation using a detailed motivation strategy.

Motivational Stratety

Motivational strategy works in a multitude of ways. Employees' best respond to "compensation programs," which is an excellent motivational factor when organizational development theory is discussed. For a "compensation program" to have significant motivational value, it must include a combination of employee options (flexible work schedules, paid time off, or overtime). Using both short - and long - term incentive components and a rather extensive mix of benefits and services allows for employees to be empowered with the organizational changes (Witt, 2000). For example, if an organization implements a change for new working hours, it is a good business practice to offer more than one work schedule for employees to select. An organization can offer a "flexible or flex-time" working schedule, with set core hours. What a "flexible or flex-time" schedule allows employees to work an 8-hour shift with an easement of coming in or leaving with in a 2-hour block of time. As long as employees work a set 8-hour shift, they have the option of coming in at 6am – 7am and leaving between 3pm – 4pm. This gives employees the ability to set an 8-hour workday with "flexible" working hours, while feeling as though they had control of their work schedules.

Organizational Development Application of Performance Management Strategies

As a human resource professional of an organization, the supportive measures of implementing organizational development and performance management strategies improvements the employee and organization efforts for growth and development. Organizational development through performance management strategies enhances employee responsibilities, knowledge, skills, efforts, and contributions vary significantly for the organization. Organizational change strategy allows for all employees and managers to take a participative involvement in the organizational development process. Performance management systems strategy ensures that all efforts are directed toward a common goal. The implementation strategy establishes a "how" in determining usefulness of the organizational changes being put in place. Lastly, the motivation strategy supplies additional methods for keeping employees motivated about the changes within the organization. When properly administered, organizational development and performance management strategies work together to improve productivity and profitability of an organization. As a human resources professional in an organization, it is important to display that the methods of using organizational development are best applied to performance management strategies by developing easy to follow steps, which are well verbalized toward the established philosophy of the organization.

Conclusion

Performance management involves senior managers in the process of developing new practices along with, communication for performance management expectations for employees, defines different activities organizations can use to better enhance organizational development. Performance management can be used as a continuous process of identifying, measuring, and developing the performance of an organizations employee. Performance management is increasingly imperative to organizational development and is becoming more inclusive in

the day-to-day tasks of the 21st century.

Introduction

Organizational leadership theories exist with the implication of creating better leaders within an organization. Organizational leadership theories vary depending on aspects of organizations and the employees that work for the organization. Employees develop organizational leadership skills from different aspects of professional and personal experiences. Some employees are "natural born" leaders, others may take some time, experience and training to develop organizational leadership skills. Organizational leadership trait theory applies to natural abilities, situational theory applies to showing leadership skills in a given situation with difficult variables and managerial organizational leadership theory outlines the purpose of supervisory and managerial leadership skills (Reese, 1995).

Trait Theory

The trait organizational leadership theory states employees have a natural ability to lead based on their personality. There are those that have a genetic natural ability to stay calm and collective while providing organizational leadership in any situation, whether it is within an organization or in their personal life. People with these traits are also said to have "out-going" personalities, along with having excellent "active listening" skills. Trait theory describes one having the ability to understand other points of view, and consideration for differences in difficult working environments. The trait theory has limitations, those that posses this ability have tendencies to also not understand how to allow for others to lead in a situation and can be overbearing. This can cause others that don't have a natural ability to lead not to want to engage interest in organizational leadership within an organization. Aspects of the trait theory, such as how to properly handle unforeseen situations and active listening skills are both examples of teachable traits employees can learn to use when developing organizational leadership skills using the trait theory.

Situational Theory

Situational theory describes the methods of designated leaders having to choose the best decisions based on the situation they are dealing with. Situational theory, suggests that all situations have numerous variables and options and within the situations there are experts to best handle them. For example, in a situation where the knowledge level of an employee was higher than of another employee, the employee with the most knowledge in the topic or subject matter would hold a greater amount of situational authority. Those who lacked the knowledge in the situation would act as supportive aspects to the authorized leader. The limitations to situational theory include changes to the variables of the situation. With changes to the situation, come possible changes in the leadership role taken. One benefit to using situational theory is it allows for other employees to gain knowledge from the situation and enhancing the organizational leadership skills of all who are evolved in the decision-making. Organizational leadership situational theory is used as a method of utilizing the organization environment as a place to develop leadership skills in employees. Currently, businesses use situational theory as a tactic to grow employee knowledge, by using "on the job training." By way of using "on the job training" employees are able to gain knowledge from experience, through a training environment (Reese, 1995).

Management Theory

Management theory is an organizational leadership theory, which focuses on the supervisor/manager role of organizational performance and development. Business management uses management theory to create leadership systems that allow for employees to be rewarded for excellent performance or reprimanded for bad performance. Employees are able to learn from the management theory through receiving feedback on work performance and evaluation of how well the work is done. For example, employees are given an annual job evaluation, where feedback is provided on what the supervisor/manager thinks of the employee's performance. Evaluations are linked to increased compensation. If the employee receives a good job evaluation, a promotion is normally the next step to show appreciate to the employee. If the employee is not up to standards, termination or demotion are options for the supervisor to suggest. Instead of only receiving annual feedback from evaluations from management, the management organizational leadership theory should implement a weekly or quarterly evaluation feedback forum for employees needing additional instruction. This will provide a method of communication between employees and managers that supersedes only getting feedback once a year (Seiden & Sowa, 2011). Either way, the management theory is effective in business management and organizational leadership practices.

Organizational Policy

As a human resource professional, crafting an organizational policy using the organizational leadership theories of trait, situational and managerial leadership skills evolve understanding the organizational structure. All organizational leadership theories have value toward developing employees in an organization, but not all theories are suited for every organization. Organizational policy for developing organizational leadership needs must include training programs for employees that may not have natural abilities, such as those stated in trait organizational leadership theory. Training programs give employees the steps to practice organizational leadership skills in the workplace. On the job training programs assist with developing employee value and work-esteem and supply a training situation for developing employee organizational leadership skills. Not all employees have the same natural abilities to handle difficult situations; "on the job training" would benefit employee organizational leadership development. Practicing in a familiar environment gives employees the understanding of possible situations, which could arise, and offers leadership skill development on making the best decisions in difficult situations.

Conclusion

A very important responsibility of any manager in an organization is to give purpose and provide direction for human effort toward developing leadership skills. When all employees are working together in a common effort with a common mission and common goals, employees'

grow and become better leaders. As employees

with different values and different behavior

patterns work together to gain leadership skills,

organizational development increases. Human

differences begin to disappear as contributions are

made and recognized. Individual strengths are

appreciated, and all employee join together to

overcome the each other's leadership weaknesses

(Reese, 1995).

References

Freedman, H. (1950). Scientific management in

    small business. *Harvard Business Review*,

    28(3), 33-53.

Reese, W. (1995). Leadership and organizational

    culture: An investigation of big ten and

    mid-american conference campus

    recreation administrations. *Journal of Sport*

    Management, *9*(2), 119-134.

Rowlinson, M. (1988). The early application of

    scientific management by cadbury.

    Business History, *30*(4), 377-395.

Seiden, S., & Sowa, J. E. (2011). Performance

management and appraisal in human service organizations: management and staff perspectives. *Public Personnel Management, 40*(3), 251-264.

Wheeler, W. (2000). Emerging organizational theory and the youth development organization. *Applied Development Science, 1,* 447-454.

Witt, U. (2000). Changing cognitive frames - Changing organizational forms: an entrepreneurial theory of organizational development. *Industrial & Corporate Change, 9*(4), 733.

www.ingramcontent.com/pod-product-compliance
Lightning Source LLC
Chambersburg PA
CBHW021039180526
45163CB00005B/2192